BEFORE TRAVELING TO ALABAMA

BEFORE TRAVELING TO ALABAMA

POEMS

DAVID ALLEN CASE

GUNPOWDER PRESS • SANTA BARBARA
2023

"Tongue-Tied" and "If I Could Rip" were previously published in *The Southern Poetry Anthology, Volume X, Alabama.*

Published by Gunpowder Press
David Starkey, Editor
PO Box 60035
Santa Barbara, CA 93160-0035

Cover image: TK

ISBN-13: 978-1-957062-09-9

www.gunpowderpress.com

For Susan Kirkland

CONTENTS

II.

III.

A Note on the Text

In 2014, I compiled and organized the poems for David Case's first book, *The Tarnation of Faust*, to highlight what seemed to me his chief concerns as a poet: his childhood and undergraduate days in Alabama; his move to and long residence in Los Angeles; the pivotal years he spent living and studying in Paris; his love for and fascination with both high and popular culture; and his final move to Florida, where he died of cardiac arrest on February 3, 2011, at the age of 49.

One of the central reasons for the founding of Gunpowder Press was to publish *The Tarnation of Faust*, and as our tenth anniversary approached, co-editor Chryss Yost and I wanted once more to honor David's memory. He had named me as his literary executor, and I selected what I thought were the best poems available for his first book; however, in rereading the many poems still unpublished, I realized there was more than enough very strong work to merit the publication of a second book.

During this period, David's sister, Susan Kirkland, sent me a digital file of his poems that she had recently discovered. In the event, I had versions of most of them already, but Susan's enthusiasm for another book by her younger brother confirmed Gunpowder's commitment to publishing a new volume of David's poetry.

Not surprisingly, many of the themes in *The Tarnation of Faust* reappear in *Before Traveling to Alabama*, a title I've borrowed from one of the new book's key poems. However, in this his second, and probably final, collection, I've allowed the poems' subject matter, like David's imagination, to roam freely, bumping up against one another more than they did in the first book. One moment a reader may be in Alabama in the 1970s, the next in Los Angeles in the 2000s. If certain poems seemed to speak to each other thematically, I've given them a little run, but David's love of wild juxtapositions within a single poem—Charlie Brown and the Champs Elysées, Sidney Poitier and the Kaiser's army in France, Bryan Ferry and the Red Cross—are on full, and brilliant, display.

As his poem "Further Meditations in an Emergency" suggests, one of David's great predecessors is Frank O'Hara, whose wry casualness and ebullient creativity can also be found in David's work. Yet, as in the poems of O'Hara, a note of sadness sounds throughout *Before Traveling to Alabama*. Writing in *The New Yorker*, Dan Chiasson notes: "The key to understanding O'Hara's 'I do this I do that' poems is in sensing the elegiac undertow that checks their forward progress." While it has been more than twelve years since his death, I still recall David's sense that even the most minor incidents were worthy of being captured in poetry, in part because he believed that tragedy loomed around every corner. His anxiety was deep, and sometimes disabling, but he fought against it with intelligence and humor. The poems in this book show David as the multifaceted person he was: sardonic and sympathetic, questioning and certain, nostalgic and forward-thinking, frightened and yet triumphant in the transformative power of his words.

—David Starkey

I.

Tongue-Tied

Speechless, I drove north into the past,
crossing the Georgia line at Madison,
heading for the nation's ugliest
near-urban tangle, Albany, Georgia, then through
the hopeless sun and clouds of Columbus,
Phenix City, and Opelika. What difference
could crossing the Tallapoosa make? Still hours
before the wine lofts of Birmingham.
That city, following the journey, looked like
Atlanta, though not for long. The
brain-eating heat held sway over
Five Points South and its eateries full
of half-despairing clients drinking whole
afternoons away, with evenings
to follow, and no soul surviving in me,
flat on my back with wine to swallow.
I looked up at Sirius, king of stars,
king of the world too, for a long while,
and the rotted wood and clammy air
refused to yield their secrets,
mocking Agee's "Sure on This Shining Night"
("High summer holds the earth..."). Holds? No, crushes
in a bear-hug, an awful wet kiss.

Floribund

Floribunda: a rose, at least a tag for one,
in the Huntington gardens,
where Mikado is all-American
and Blue Boy Christmas ornaments
sell briskly to Asians in the gift shop.

I was once Floribund myself,
marooned on that flat peninsula.
I saw the Keys, where America dissolves.
Six-toed cats, lizards in kitchen sinks,
a "Bears of Southwest Florida" convention:
Oh the dancing hairy men!
The islands curled toward Mexico, out of sight.
I sloshed in the water warm as soup, toed the pasty sand.
My marriage melted in the heat of walks
at 6:00 a.m. in the pseudo-city Tampa
with its collapsed bay bridge unrepaired
and undemolished. All the roses were sick
and the Wal-Mart gun shop closed
two hours later than the pharmacy.

Une Promesse de Bonheur

The gods, the gangs, the family, imaginings:
it doesn't matter what you call them.
You know when they've had it with you.
You call and wait at doctors' offices
desperate to be seen and touched,
crying for the needles that will wreck
your veins for months or ages.

The car knocks at full speed, and not
at heaven's door; the lark ascends
but can't find heaven's gate. Birds
of a certain feather pick at your flesh—
and what could ever scare a daw?
Clearer and clearer comes the vision
of what to leave behind, while vaguer

than ever is the thought of what will greet you.
If only I'd given my pathetic life
and its puny reflection on Facebook
to the ukulele: I seriously doubt
that Jake Shimabukuro has ever
had a doubt about anything,
while who's ever seen a happy

piano player in a movie?
We know the secret of the player
in *The Specter of the Rose*. Those weren't
the days, either. Sonji Kimmons at
The Other Side has her own secret:
she knows what love is, you don't.
What else does F-minor have to say?

All college football heads north,
leaving us with carping tailgate parties,
the bitterness that wins so easily.
Do you remember the dinner
in the absurd steakhouse where
the neon worm crawled out of the parsley?
We laughed at it, being happy anyway.

If I Could Rip

If I could rip the heart from a quintet
of Schumann's, could then step back
to see the arteries and tendons pull

it in to the place required by
Leonardo's famous sketch (displayed
by a pizza joint, then taken down

because of public scandal) or by
Mozart's balanced instincts, I would know
everything that poetry could teach us. I

realize that Mozart is not Brahms:
the ripping Brahms always demands
for his aged, masochistic flesh is

different in kind and kith from Mozart's
foreplay and caresses, the climax
spread throughout the movement so that

everything is touched with love. Both
things are love, and few can understand
two kinds of love, most never knowing one.

I can rip away the hostile mask over
my Mozart-loving face only in these ways:
devotion to these marks on scores and pages,

remembering kissing Anthony's eyes.

In the Unlikely Event of a Landing at Sea

In the unlikely event of a landing
at sea, instead of the familiar
New Orleans International,
we will be braced for impact,
ready to use the seat cushion
as flotation device, ready
for the post-hurricane season nip
of the salty, muddy, oily Gulf.
You will remain calm there,
awaiting Coast Guard vessels,
hydroplaning in Tom Swift fashion,
fresh from a tour of drug-
interdiction and immigrant hunting.
The clean-cut, drawling officers
will offer you a plate of blackened snapper.

No, you will prepare for death, the uncertainties
of the task being no impediment:
the lines of the Hail Mary will alternate
with curses, with the life
that "flashes before one's eyes," even
the afternoon at the mechanic's,
the wasteland of San Fernando Road,
the shouting Armenians.

Who has found shelter in flotation cushions?
Show me, that I might have faith.

Visions of Christ in Malibu

The cashier and the drink-maker
are talking eagerly about a book. I
astonished ask what the book might be.
The cashier explains that it's a Christian book
about *really becoming a man*. It
bases its ideas, he says, largely
on Mel Gibson's character in *Braveheart*—
also, no doubt, the scene in which
Edward throws his son's smiling lover out
the window in a royal tower.
(When I saw it, the crowd laughed
like the partiers in "Revolution 9.")
The drunk-driving anti-Semite Gibson—
far more Catholic even than Benedict—
is now pope of dopey Protestants.

Virile religion mutates
at thrice the old rate in upper Malibu,
the estate beneath the Serra retreat
that a pipe-smoking Franciscan pointed at.
The Spirit arrives in Florida in a flash.
Now the kid is sweeping up
behind my table, glancing at what
I write, growing in wisdom with the dust.
He'd never mentioned Jesus, maybe
because Gibson had crucified him.
Could these hearty boys follow a rabbi, after all?

Bible

Byblos, book, a hundred books
with three hundred writers, trimmed
by bishops and Byzantines.
Almost all of Aristotle erased
to make room for the procession
taking the gilded text down the incensed aisle: "This
is the Word of the Lord!" though most
come from crazed shepherds and the star-struck
misremembered—to be continued
by Paul's "I hope the knife slips."

Deluxe volumes "suitable for throwing
purposes," as Saint Dorothy remarked;
old Gutenbergs, Vulgates, Douays, King James-
es, Revised Standards, Gideons, Jerusalems,
translators dreading or drooling over the approach
of Ezekiel, chapter twenty-three.

Bibliophile

He stands alone in an ancestral house
now bare of furnishings. He is quite thin
from his diet: licking the vellum
on his books, which are *rarissimi*.

When he is done licking the vellum,
he eats his hands finger by finger,
punishing himself for being the last
of a line as aristocratic as The Addamses.

Books published in Venice especially
excite him—the binding, the paper,
the locks, folds, and printers' touches.
He has a mantle without gewgaws, the wall

perfectly bare, the formerly shadowed parts
adding a *presque rien* of the post-modern.
He may have a vague interest in de Sade,
but tosses it to the would-be, the dullards.

Older Sister

Now I picture her
alone in her dark house
with the heavily draped windows
in a subdivision
feeding a rabbit instead of a dog
or cat

Her cheery talk and her laugh
always screamed out something
held in
badly

She worries her pulse
ever higher
crying and thinking about
our mother

At least she is brave
enough to think

She stands
between me
and that
catastrophe

The Idiot's Guide to Peace

As America is shopping, I
sit at a tiled Moorish garden-table
listening to a jazzy rendition of *Dona
Nobis Pacem* ("grant us peace," from the Latin,
as if the Romans knew anything about it).
I confess to drinking a soy latte.
The newspaper plays down
the brewing war with North Korea
in favor of Black Friday specials
and that annual *temblor* Alabama-
Auburn—or Auburn-Alabama.
The opposite of étiquette it is, though

I see books on manners five feet away.
Where is the book on peace? The owner
can't find it, just notes and musings
of the reigning pope, the one
who wants to beatify—so many write
beautify—Pius the Terrible,
I mean The Twelfth, a.k.a. Hitler's Pope.

The DJ switches to an instrumental
'lude from "The Sound of Music." The hills
are alive therewith.
                    Meanwhile,
the aircraft carrier George Washington
is steaming east to protect
our interests in The China Sea.

Another Mule's Been Kickin' in Yer Stall

Striking turns of phrase, bolts from
the heavens, great metaphors
are given to any, though seldom
to those who crave them: more often to those
who live like poets, wandering
the roads, obeying Baudelaire ("Be always drunk"),
not being particular about where they piss.
Read Ezekiel 23 if you don't
believe me, study the writing
of prostitutes—and don't neglect
elegies for the zombies. Take
"Jesusland": a hymn for all the poor in spirit
came perfectly, dead on arrival.
Look how much more it says than *Elmer Gantry*
did. Compare Frost's long poems (early
and late) with the swift "Provide, provide!"
which would be still more merciless
did it not recall Gomer Pyle's "Surprise! Surprise!"

Elizabeth Taylor Tweets from Hospital Bed

At once cat-like and bird-like, she lies,
famed for her failures but bigger than them.
She has been sweet and sour, maybe
better at sour, maybe at her best
throwing bitter words and whisky glasses.

Getting a little forgetful, sometimes
she has to count them: myself, I lost
count twenty years ago. The guy
from rehab took it to a different level,
of course, and then she sold her passion.

What's with her now? Why is it
so hard to think of her as bed-ridden,
wheelchair-riding, dumped somewhere,
left twittering and regretful,
yet somehow expensive and imperial?

Blasted

Not the sort of punishment
one expects at the end, more like nitrogen
narcosis—rapture of the deep,
the bends. And our final conversation
was less like the curiosa
found on the back shelves of adult
bookstores, more like the weary
sophisticated talk of Nobel laureates ten years after
their awards, when, no longer
feted, they still expect
daily acclaim.

I felt blasted that morning, just totally shot.
Brown bottles of Sierra Nevada pale ale
stood sentry on the nightstand around
a bottle of Belladonna, your scent. Some things
I couldn't quite figure out:
Where he'd gone, or why.
The Venus's-flytrap on the windowsill was droopy and yellowing,
hadn't trapped a fly in weeks.

Look, I've come down
from my ivory tower already, give me a break. I sold
my CD collection for gas money and now this.
My tongue tasted like library paste, my life had been carried
to its *reductio ad absurdum*.
The phone rang and I let it.
I'd tell you the exact date if you wanted to know.
What defines an act of bravery? Answer me that and I swear
I'll tell you what happened next.

Reading Tennessee

Something's slurping up my serotonin,
nobody is sleeping in my bed
except the sedated version
of myself. Don't tell me that,
in Iraq, things would be worse:
The Times today said Iraqi gays
are "scorned and murdered"—in that order.

Americanization is working.

Here, upstanding citizens are always voting
on me, debating me, now and then embracing me.
Petitions and court orders, recalls, recounts:
five jokes on each sitcom episode
scream with derision. Who's really the cat
on the hot tin roof? Skipper's love
for Brick kills Skipper, Skipper's death
kills Brick. I feel heavy in the loafers.

Nothing in Particular

When it hit me that I loved you,
that *maturity* made so little difference,
I pounded the senseless steering wheel:
Shit! Shit! I can't believe it! SHIT! Later,
when I'd put a decent face on things,
knowing you'd never be back to sing
like an angel landed next to me (I've been
burned by your sort too often anyway...),
I saw between the rows of music stands
a half-full water bottle you'd handed me
to sip from two weeks before.

Anywhere You Go

Gin Blossoms, 1995

You wrote me a letter, and I trembled,
then rejoiced, on opening it. (Yes, from you,
doomed to be archbishop of Paris.)
May I dream of you again, sent down
by as many drugs, as much wine, as it takes,
but I'll settle for fatigue and lassitude
to lead me back to you, the memory
of sex adding to the décor
while never disturbing the order
or the beauty. I love you for that:
I can "follow you down" and never get lost,
never feel trapped or close.

Like Keats's Autumn, you hang your head
and seldom show your face. Pity me,
one of the cursed who must see it
now, in this world, especially yours, where
it's most likely to appear.
It isn't a bad time to die, the whole world
shopping, the sun now out of the picture.

Poem

Fall in Love said the magazine
in the clinic waiting room
so I looked through all of Google Earth
for Compatible Partners

the procurers offered men
who loved "antiquing and gyming"

They said they were passionate
about seventeen little things
especially about LIFE   all of it
the Dollar Generals and Books a Millions

Life the tune-ups and electrical outages
the pre-game sports talk Marie Osmond dolls
hiking in the smog infomercials
for erectile dysfunction

passionate about everything indirect rebuke
of my cold eye   my calibrated medication
two glasses of Malbec with every dinner

Loaves and Fishes

Going up the coast on Labor Day
is a mistake. We turn inland,
go up the 101 to San Francisco.
When we get there, it is midnight.
Everything is full and throbbing.
Over to Berkeley to stay
at the Durant Hotel, just uphill
from Telegraph. We sleep deeply
till the sun is swimming in the curtains.
We walk downhill to breakfast
and see my friend Mark, my workmate
in LA. I introduce him to Alan,
but they know each other well,
it seems. (They didn't know they both
knew me; it is almost like Facebook.)
The rest of the weekend we spend
with Mark (and Massimo Porrati),
driving up and down the Berkeley Hills
in rain and fog listening to the only tape
we have, Sting's "Nothing Like the Sun."
Something in the fog and rain is heavenly.
Every day another miracle, only death...

At night we head for The City, getting on
the Bay Bridge. Then traffic stops for a long time.
Folks turn off their engines and get out.
We pass around the beer and pot,
it multiplies. Suddenly,
this hulking bridge is human.

For a better view, Mark and I walk
to the edge to look at the city
and blow smoke at the Bay. We
see tremendous ships docked by
Potrero Hill, look back at Oakland,
wondering what's there without the Raiders.
Cars start starting and we jump back in,
ending up at a tedious dance club
where Massimo and I sing Proust's praises.
The next thing I remember,
Mark and Alan and I are driving
through the Tejon Pass, another
bridge, but this time over solid
fault-scarred rock. I have since failed
to die there several times: wind,
snow, breakdown.
I have been asleep
a very long time. I see they were lovers
once. They argue like a couple
in Stage Four, wrangle top and bottom
over who's to blame. They forget
that there's a child in back.

Evensong

Another whistle, another "Joto!"
or "Faggot!" I really shouldn't walk
so much—it endangers my health—
neither should I stay home: the neighbors
saw me kissing my date good night
and they've made up a song about it.

It goes "Honk," "beep," basketball
bouncing high outside my windows, slamming doors
when I go in or out. (There's never
music for this song, may God be thanked.)
The shouts, true to type, come mainly
from pickup trucks and vans that drive off
quickly: they are cowards! *Que dieu soit loué.*
Once, a pickup shouted at my straight brother
and me as we emerged from a liquor/
grocery on Russian Hill: tourists, I'll bet.

I forgot to mention the whistles.
A smidgen of hope remains.
The Lord is kind and merciful,
We used to sing at outdoor guitar mass—
We even half believed it. *The Lord is kind.*

Asking for It

In the fortieth June after Stonewall,
Fort Worth police observed the date
scrupulously: they stormed into the Rainbow
Room oinking incoherent orders,
clubbing patrons on the head, the back, the stomach.
'R you looking at me, faggot? one said, *Suck
on this for a change*—though it
was clear that nothing had changed.
That was the message. This new line was confirmed
by the Police Chief's communiqué:
That faggot was asking for it—the faggot
in question having been taken
to Emergency with a blood-clot
on his brain. Twenty patrons
lined up outside in hand-cuffs
recalled that they were in a 'burb
of Dallas, Texas, a unique blend
of the worst of the South with the worst
of the West. Sobbing, one man said,
"They hate us. After all these years,
they still hate us." Nobody told him.

II.

Black Felt Hat

I was a kid with a winning
broken grin, but the day I saw
I was twenty pounds lighter
than my classmates, my decline
began. At fourteen I was CTD.
My nose grew as despondent
as my too-thin lips. At eighteen,
I was loved only because another organ
had grown outsized. It mocked the rest
of my body.
                    So, when Alan and I
moved to The Melrose (it was The Melrose
then), I expected little of its Hip
to rub off on me.
                              As we walked east
one morning, though, the heavens
opened: a clothing store called Aardvark's.
We went in, feeling the threads, not
meaning to buy, but in back we saw hats.
One of them was the hat John Lennon
wore on the cover of "Hey Jude," an LP
singles collection we'll never see again.
The hat was mine, at any cost: I
clapt it on when we were outside.
Five seconds later, an open car
made a squealing U-ie to draw beside us.
"WHERE did you GET that HAT?" the driver
yelled. I pointed to the magic store.

Visiting home that August, my brother
was floored. "Dave, that is

the ULTIMATELY cool hat!"
His coolest friend summoned me
to his mountain.
                    In clubs and bars,
at parties, men and women hovered,
asking to dance with the hat and me.

One terrible day ten months later,
I fell in love, in that slavish manner
that, this time, became abject:
I wanted (why?) to become this man.
So many parties, concerts, colloquies
later, we were dancing to Brian Ferry's
"Limbo"—we being several. I ended
up with one woman, who begged
for it. The man was there, watching. What
could I have done? I let her wear it:
I saw that it became her.
She was new, brilliant, attached.
Leaving, she removed it, reluctantly
tendered it: He was watching.
I told her, "It's yours," and He exclaimed,
"What a guy!"
The highest praise
was all the love I won from him.

She and the hat vanished into the courtyard,
The Melrose, Hollywood, LA, the County,
the desert and the valleys down in Limbo.

Yeshu

This is the Hebrew form, sounding
like a sneeze. "Yeshu, God bless you." It's
Iesus Nazarenus Rex Iudaeorum,
to quote from Pilate's post-it,
but Latin loses the eloquent Y,
arms stretched out, head hanging broken
this time, no baptism, no magician's dove,
heaven closed with a black drape.
So Yeshu cries *Fait accompli!*
on snifting the myrrh and vinegar,
resigned to the departure
of the Ghost.
That Ghost now parts
with no regret, taking the high road,
wishing to be worshiped in Spirit and in Truth.
Those towns are very far from here.

Georges Rouault, Head of Christ (Los Angeles County Museum)

On Not Being Jewish

It happened one night as I was crossing
Fairfax at Santa Monica Boulevard
in East West Hollywood:
                                    Two young men
in black wool suits and hats asked politely,
as quietly as the traffic allowed, "Sir,
is your mother Jewish?" Oddly phrased,
to be sure—or perhaps they saw enough
to know there was little of my father
in me. I smiled sadly and shook
my head: "No, not Jewish." Yes,
I know the definition is matrilineal
and, apparently, inflexible.
Still, I was scandalized a little:
Why *couldn't* I be Jewish? Why not Jewish,
skeptic, Catholic, Buddhist all at once?
                                            I'd

been to a Jewish wedding—lesbian
couple, lesbian rabbi, seen in broken
glass the irrevocable union,
but I was just the piano player.
The chief rabbi, though, had *Parsifal*,
in full orchestral score, on his piano.
If he could inhabit Wagner, couldn't I dwell
in Mahler—the 2nd Symphony,
the *Kindertotenlieder*?

I too live in an unquiet house.

A Christmas Carol

In the beginning, none of us could tell
her hallucinations from the truth.

Last week in Alabama, rain was beating
on the pavilions at the graveyard.
We were standing on dead cousins
hearing the preacher's uncomforting words:
"She is not in heaven now
because she was a good, sweet woman..."
Yes, she is, you fool. If anyone is.

Guests came with baskets, casseroles,
and (the greatest tribute) seven pecan pies.
By some miracle of politeness,
no one spoke of football for hours.

Two days later, my father, my brother, and I
drove to an ancient mining town
with a small Russian church.
We wondered if there were a word
for an onion-shaped spire.
We drove further, past one
Free Will Baptist church, then another,
then a foreign-car junkyard.
The South in winter has neither white nor green
to cover the crying shame of it all.
Christmas will be well spent away.

We were always prone to venerate.
I crush a coffin rose inside a novel.

Salvation Army

This benevolent society
has sent a tone-deaf woman to wail
Christmas carols and jingles
and to make her ugly bell tinkle
for every Publix customer.
It is November 22, the Saint's Day
of a president whose wife dressed well.

Thanksgiving is near, remote families
will be spewed out and drawn in like
the fountains at California Plaza.
This year, the football is to die for.
Age of the Concussion. Focus on
the Torn Tendon. Hate in the Christian air.

I could make a list. If I made lists.
Inventories? Résumés?
Rejection can be beautiful, but
no one to love?
                        At a small party
twenty-five years ago, a plain-
spoken rube broke in and foretold
all this: "You'll end up alone,
every single one of you:
you're just too exclusive."

He was "right," though he's still a crude-ass
closet case, maybe still alone himself.

Tomorrow night, the Peanuts kids
will sing "Christmas Time Is Here."
They're not even close. I want my twelve days back.

Germans in Champagne

I write this missing the presentation
of *Raisin in the Sun* (with Poitier)
I'd meant to watch, so let's go
to Poitier, one of those hundreds
of stinking pyrrhic victories
in which the soldiers of a king
gleefully killed the soldiers
of a cousin of their nation's king.
One book said Tours was really Poitier;
now I'm not sure about it, but
the grapes there were juicy,
especially the red ones, the ones
that, through well-made paintings, made
people think that Rome declined and fell
because a reclining Nero ate too many.

In World War I, the Germans occupied
Champagne and thought they were in heaven.
Maybe they were right, but they didn't know
what to do with heaven. Talking
Heads said heaven is a place
"where nothing, nothing ever happens."
They and the Buddha agree.

So we have all loved each other from the start;
if only we had known. These long wars—
I know now they're completely phony, though
most folks don't know how to live without them.

Rue des Blancs Manteaux

The men in shining raiment, the youth
who fled, leaving his white garment
in rough and clueless Roman hands,
Lazarus instructed in the mysteries
of heaven, mysteries so heavenly
the very mention is excised from all
except Mark's secret gospel:
you are defamed by the infernal clan
of bishops, cardinals, and bible
salesmen, by the well-intentioned saints.
And so is God defamed, detached
from love, subject and predicate reversed.
Untie the knots, remove the hood
in which God's been travestied, let out
the blazing light, the Bang, the white heat
leaving its trace even on a street-sign
in cold, stony-streeted Paris.

Aux Champs-Elysées!

I've left my Gazebo of Despair
forever, led on by my student's "pencils
of uncertainly" that draw me
farther along Moonshine Creek Trail,
lunar in its bowls of dust.
There's a small stream for mixing bread,
a tarn where there should
be alligators (but there are none),
a stunted tree at a crossing still
hanging with shards of "autumn coloration"
like stained glass when the Lutherans
were finished with it, or like the Christmas tree
Charlie Brown has chosen before Linus
and Pigpen smother it with dirty love.
Suddenly, I am possessed with music,
singing *Il y a tout c'que vous voulez*
aux Champs Elysées...Aux Champs Elysées!
whistling the horn riffs between the lines
that are so Carnival-procession-like, so
like David dancing the Ark to the Holy City.

Montréal

It was exactly as I'd feared: you
really were "more English than the Queen,"
though your French was fluent, as your mother
required. You took such devoted care
of her, I could tell how deep your hatred ran.
You could go almost for two hours
without some kind of bitter tea (ten dollars
a cup in the hippest part of town).

Of course, nothing could prepare me
for the dénouement: the midnight
when you burst into my room
not for love, but to take the heater
you'd so kindly provided
off the floor, smashing with it
my old college baseball cap: some
echo had disturbed you below stairs.

It wasn't that you couldn't hold your liquor; you
couldn't hold your Kir!

I said nothing the night after, nothing
on the drive to the airport, or in farewell.
You called, as *you* would, to demand a report.
I sent it the next day. Sharp, scornful, it did the trick.

As for the city, it seemed nice enough,
and I brought back five books from Gallimard.

Monopoly

The great game required little skill:
the gods decided everything,
down to the Depression-era icons—
iron, shoe, top hat, and thimble.
We worked mightily to buy
as many plots of land as needed
to keep the others from finding
home, or even rest. We rejoiced at others'
bankruptcies and incarcerations,
their payment of luxury taxes
when short on cash, their pathetic
efforts to raise an empire
from Baltic Avenue or Marvin Gardens.
Half the time, they couldn't pass Go!
We saw fat men collapse from bank errors
"in their favor," not from shrunken trusts
or twisted mortgages and debt kept "off the book."
It was all dull-as-dishwater true, not like
the transparent fraud of Electric Football,
Hotwheels, or ant-like toy soldiers.
And the gods? They're sipping Cristal again.

Facebook I

Prepare a face: is your photo catching? Are
your interests paying off? Do you show
well that you aren't taking this too seriously?
You wouldn't really agree to take any
of those fatuous quizzes, would you?
I can't be tagging friends at my age;
surely I have more important things
to do. Or do I? "You know I could never
be alone." Separation anxiety:
keep your friends close and distant à la fois.
Think what Henry James could have done
in this medium.

Facebook II

There will be time, there will be time...

My profile needs some tweaking.
I don't see the right balance
between sophistication
and absurdity, between
high and low. I hear Bowie
singing *Facebook!* [turn] *Facebook!*
[turn], see Old Prufrock fretting.

I left "About Myself" blank
because it seemed redundant.
My faves are so *over*, my
date-of-birth anchored so far
back in a pre-history
when people got up from where
they sat to change the station

on the Motorola. I
check each hour to see who,
who, may have commented
on my latest post, and how.
"Famous People You Have Met,"
"Which Celebrity Should You
Marry?" "Which Political

Theorist Are You?" Should I
accept an IQ challenge
("One Friend thinks that you are dumb!")
embedded in a cell phone

promo/data collection
scheme? I can't lose face: this is
called FACE-book, right? Discretion's

needed for throwing faces
out there, particularly
the faces of one's Friends: Who
yet hasn't looked them over
to cull the really top-notch
from piddling acquaintances,
the dregs of our former lives?

Facebook III

"I was de-friended!" I heard
one guy saying, aware both
of the affront and of his
testing novel linguistic
terrain. True desolation,
being de- or un-friended,
off the guest list, lost, and shunned.

And then, the former lovers,
distant, present, everywhere:
a near-miss kiss-kiss seems all
that's wise, but even that speaks
volumes. Note exhibits A,
B, and C, bad sends, Comments
never erased, just hidden.

Yet quiet's only for the
coolest: I could never sit
still, as a Friend once noted
in a book closed long ago
but just re-opened. May god
pity me: I surrender!
Will my real friends please stand up?

Facebook IV (Losing Face)

This Face-Book can make you shrink, or cringe.
The old advice ("no religion or politics")
doesn't compute: one of your fifty friends
or one of their sixty friends apiece
will break the code, some calling Kennedy
the Last Great Man and others—you can guess.
All anti-anger mantras evaporate
in the heat of the Health Care Smack-Down.

No one was persuaded, someone sang,
or should have. (Was it Dylan?)
From sneers to sadness to sneers.
We'll die not knowing how it happened
that the world went to war—again—for a lie.

Farewell to Lunch

A long ta-ta—hello lightheaded hell
in which each step and pen-stroke
records the half-life of a skeleton
(as here with "Passion" tea, oat cookie,
a *New York Times* hopelessly behind
the news cycle) having bare memories
of the really fine Jane Austen film,
the Empire waists causing every woman
to seem to be concealing a pregnancy.
My old friend, a terribly sweet guy,
has just told me his life has gone
to anger at biology and DNA
(by which he means his ex-wife).
All the lines I've ever written
or spoken don't add up to a good jazz song,
and this cup with the Starbucks imprimatur
has barely pierced the fog of dreams and oversleep.

Slipping Under

Something in me is fighting
to wake up, as if I'd been
half-cured of wakefulness
by adding a second sleep to the one
I've almost always had. But
what if wakefulness (the kind
the Buddha had) is ill-conceived,
what if the happiest creatures
are the sloth and the trilobite?
I could wake up and hear nothing
but the Beach Boys forever—hell,
yes, but not the worst of hells.
There are always Supertramp
and The Starland Vocal Band.

I Open My Wormy Heart

Masahiko said—when I was twenty-two—
that I had a warm heart, and remembering
his delusion almost warms my heart.
But they don't age well, these warm hearts.
Nothing sillier than those cheesy Jesus
pictures of the Sacred Heart, the plunge inside
the bloody chest. Weeping angel, help me weep.

As for you, sun of my soul, distance
drew you near, while one step towards you
worked a miracle: you vanished.
For three days, I've been bleeding,
coughing, shivering like Tom on the heath—
except that here is cold climate control,
the feel of unwarmed metal on the back.

Two Waiting Rooms

1.
The TV here's playing "I Love Lucy,"
an episode in which some Cubans visit Ricky.
Ethel tries her Spanish: *¿Como estan?*
This provokes excited talk,
to which Ms. Mertz can answer only *Oui.*
The farce is perfect, and all
the Mexican patients laugh at once,
from two sides of the neutral tongue.
We are all drinking contrast fluid
hoping for high-definition tumors.
Before we know it, Lucy has turned
into the Maharincess of Franistan.

2.
This is the surgeon's recovery room.
After my neck is cut and stitched,
I am left alone, radio on Coast 104
with Whitney Houston: she will always love me.
Wham! and Lionel Ritchie follow.
When the Peruvian Gregorio comes to roll me
to my family, I see the shining path ahead
and I remember reading, as a kid,
about the burning at the stake of Atahualpa,
the last Incan emperor.
The Spanish offered him beheading
in exchange for his conversion.
He did not want to go to heaven.

The Pale

Given: I'm beyond it. Turns out, though,
there are many pales, many chances
to add the "too" to "much" or "far,"
the "de" to "trop," the very *demasiado*—
God's given me the habit of doing
it, the bent for missing the chalk lines
or markers that prevent the solo march,
the single file, the mistaken melody
that lasts five beats after cut-off.
Indeed, I am far too pale. Even
as I lay on the hospital table,
my neck barely sewn up,
the doctor said, "David, you're just too much."
And so it was confirmed, by the best opinion.
The next thing I knew, I was alone,
"recovering," in a metallic chamber.

Further Meditations in an Emergency

"Don't just do something, sit there!"
—Anonymous

Yes, there is no more to venture forth with,
no dune buggy having intervened,
no MOMA between me and the stone.
In memory of my feelings, though,
there is the book from MOCA's show
dedicated to you and the New York
artists of the fifties and sixties,
strangely but fitly mounted
in Los Angeles nine years ago,
as it came time for the rest of my life,
as now it comes again, again, surprising.

III.

Before Traveling to Alabama

State of tornadoes and electoral chicanery,
you seem farther and stranger
than ever twenty years after I left.
James stayed, he told me, because "It's so easy
to be cool here," meaning
he didn't have to work at it, or much of anything.
I almost stayed myself, I almost
got sucked into the myth, the Spanish moss,
the disquieting ghosts of river Chickasaw
and Seminole, doomed French and Spanish outposts
manned by the dregs of the empires.
Did I forget the evil? If you can take the stench,
the evil is charming, always crumbling richly,
never vanishing quite without a trace.
If you can take the Klan, pickups
with rifle racks, and lots of Lynyrd Skynard,
the mountains are mighty in autumn;
the football chants are magic
until the whisky winds down. Everyone will ask
which church you belong to and size you up right there: they
will place your accent, too, down to the county line.
You can see them thinking "Black Belt,"
"Cajun," "South Georgia," or "almost Yankee."
Be glad you can pay at the pump these days.

Los Angeles

I drive under the sign, the disembodied
names, the compelling arrows, drawing
me seventy miles per hour into
the swarm, the city of the plain and mountain;
desert and ocean, arrows plunging
into my heart, which is delighted end-
lessly by the foreign grown familiar
in Anglo-Spanish-Korean Little Armenia
Thai Town, Monterey Park briefly Anglo,
briefly Latino again,
now Chinese, but "they think they're still
in Kiev," as Larry Roth once said
about the Fairfax, where Russians in exile
grow gayer as they mount the hill
toward the west of Hollywood like a tidal wave
of deco onto Fountain, briefly posh,
meandering east until it turns
into Hyperion of bars and gyms
and sushi before surging across
the LA River, trees breaking stubbornly
the concrete bed until we have what look
like Roman ruins, sky marbled blue
and white, light fog coming from nowhere
after sunset to provide some atmosphere
for the Rolling Stones, who play tonight downtown
and who could use soft-focus
after this many shows, this many parties
in the hills, so much first- and second-hand smoke.

—November 2, 2002

Los Feliz, Fire Season

Pies are happy food, and happiness is ignoble.
Just look at those pie-filled people
discreetly seated in the rear
at The Alcove. When I was last there,
I saw a friend, a distant friend—for
they can be as distant as relatives—
who was thin like a real poet, with deep
purple eyes and delicate lids, the pupils
permanently dilated from...
I didn't want to ask. He had obviously
found some good shit. He even had
an Italian name.
                    He was alone,
living in North Hollywood. How had things
come to that? He was fighting with neighbors,
he was bitterer than I, and swifter.
I wanted to stroke his hair and tell him
he had to change his life, but nothing
so facile made sense, after seeing
Moon Pies offered for six dollars
when they are simply tossed from floats
to rooting rednecks at Mardi Gras
in Mobile. (I'll make myself ill,
for Christ's sake.) A few blocks away,
an All State Insurance commercial
is being filmed at Café Figaro, where
coq au vin comes without the least
influence from wine. As
for my friend, he seems to want everything
that he hates, even more life, even
the praise of those he despises.

Branchings

The phone ringing in the next room
will follow one of many branches: it
is a sibling announcing a divorce

or death; it is a suicidal friend
from high school urging my return,
a small-time credit offer from a bank

in Georgia, a collector looking
for the owner of the long-defunct
El Mexicano Market, unwilling

to believe I have no connection
to the place; it is a reproachful
artist in Orange County angry

that we in Los Angeles are not
sending missionaries to their aid;
a doomed mayoral candidate who reminds

me that "the children are the future,"
an ex-boyfriend hoping that the past
was better than it seemed at the time.

Variations on a Text of Langston Hughes

"I was saved from sin when I was going on thirteen. But not really.
It happened like this."

I was baptized when I was eight,
but not really. It was a Baptist church
where my mother loved the music, but
the lyrics and the sermons had me
thinking I'd be "left behind," all that talk
of blood, wormwood, fire, temptation
connected somehow to Mutual Assured
Destruction and my C on a third-grade
math exam the week before. Every
thunder clap meant the opening
of a Seventh Seal, or a trumpet blast,
and, worse still, silence
"for the space of an hour."

One night

I ran to the front of the church, embarrassed
and relieved. I said that I wanted to be
saved, to be baptized, even though
baptism was no guarantee of anything.
There was never a guarantee, just evidence
the guarantee had been withdrawn.
So why be baptized Baptist? I never asked.

After a lost week, I was walking into
the baptismal water—the pool was warm,
my heart beating faster and harder. As I
approached the minister, he hissed my name:

DAvid, what are you DOing?
He blenched. I was pissing in the water.
The not-quite-sacrament went on. He lowered
me into the tainted water in the name
of The Big Three. Did I believe? Did he?
Was God cursing me, as when he cursed
Pharaoh, and the Nile ran red for Yul Brenner?

For forty years I kept quiet, but just last night
I told my brother, who laughed his head off.

Birmingham Museum

A viscountess preserved by Sargent
presides over a riot of influences.
Tearful partings between Confederate
officers and their slaves.
Paul Robeson. G.W. Carver welcomed
by FDR. Across the street,
a wing for contemporary Japanese.

Another *Head of John the Baptist*
(Rodin) turns up.
                    One Italian half-master
has taken Botticelli's cheekbones
and made the faces more sinister.

A Creek village without Creeks.
Bathing beauties snapped by Arbus.
Saint George and his eternal dragon
in wood ready for kindling.

A Note for Wallis Simpson

I'm now hungry enough to understand
those who just can't eat enough—who need
the hearty breakfast with its stack
of fried batter slathered in honeyed butter
with a side of bacon and gravy,
the All-You-Can-Eat buffets taken
at their word, the hidden snacks,
seconds at dinner with a Chocolate
"Blackout Cake" to follow, the chips
and mango salsa, consumed
while watching The Food Channel, dreaming
of trips to New Orleans or Lyon
to perfect their gourmandise—but
we should not despise their dreams.
We're all pressured to incorporate,
to consume with increasing confidence.
After all, art is hunger—or a feast.
The German word for death is *starve*.
Only the dead are, as my students write, "too cool to eat."

Boozing Camilla Liver Transplant

Some things write themselves, the cynic
on autopilot dreaming of Berlioz
and the ultra-blue sky while in line
at Publix Supermarket, headed for
the neighborhood liquor store to buy
Southern Comfort for a performance
of Mozart's *The Impresario.*
Someone's already writing *Camilla: The Opera*
in which the protagonist bounces the servants
so she can drink freely from the bottle
and sing like Iphigenia of her cursed
family, of "the woe that is in marriage."
There's ice in her thin blue veins
that only someone else's parts can melt. Her
robes and ornaments drag on her tired limbs.
She draws a warm bath for her dashing old prince.

Words for Mary

Accepting an award that, if one
used the vocabulary of Dick Cheney,
might be called a "no-brainer," you,
Mary Leontyne Price, kindly exaggerated
the award's importance.
                      Thin-boned and -fleshed,
you spoke a bit, and then bestowed
a greater honor on the audience,
singing briefly, convincingly,
in the higher octave. You were eighty-one.
Your cheeks were rouged for the backmost
and topmost seats, your eyes circled
in thick mascara, making the picture
of tragedy, eyes now twice as large
as life.
        Your Met début had come the year
John Kennedy took office, the year
when I was born to promises of greatness
that were seldom kept. You powered on.
Imagine a prime-time broadcast of Poulenc's
"Dialogues of the Carmelites" on a major
network, featuring you as Madame Lidoine!

I wonder what you think, perhaps alone,
happening upon *American Idol* while
surfing the TV spectrum with dying hopes.

The Diaries

Of course I'm reading them twenty years
too late for you to see any point
in my reading them—that's a given.
What position could I have held
in your factory? You're a New York
standard, but you said "the best parties"
had all the folk from Europe and Hollywood.
Delectably shallow, right down to the cab fares
and hotel tips, a Proust in mental collapse,
you retouched photos of anyone
over twenty and you "worked" (at what?)
in the afternoons, till the cab fares
and parties and dinners began again:
one day, three hours "lost" figuring
out where to eat. That's an art, too,
though there's usually just one answer:
La Grenouille, unless it's a rich family
treating guests to dog food spooned out
by six servants. Mick Jagger slept
in your bed, drunk as a lord, while
you took out Bianca or looked for
crab-removal systems. Surprisingly,
you found none in Kuwait, where the royals
had a monopoly. "You think about paint,
you think about glue..." you spend
ninety minutes signing people's cans.
Strange to see that you went to mass,
got down on your knees, and prayed
for money—and maybe other things
though I guess that's where you learned
that something very simple takes a turn
for the luminous, that even Brillo boxes
are brilliant under industrial lights.

The Great American Novel

It will open with a fight to the death
between Charles Bronson and Gina Lolla-
brigida. James Baldwin will read
his posthumous *Lamentations*
and DeLillo'll recount the Kennedy
assassination from a coffeehouse
called The Grassy Knoll, just down from
Tang's Doughnuts, at Sunset and Fountain.
The Producer who knows what he wants
will finally know how to spell it.
Somebody important in Congress
will commit hari-kiri one hundred sixty years
late over passage of the Fugitive Slave Act.
Katherine Anne Porter will visit
Lafitte in Exile, leaving a permanent
wrinkle in her nose not unlike that
in Elizabeth Montgomery's, who will
finally explain The New Darrin.
Somebody in New England
will be in an excellent mood.

No Outlet

Someone cleaning out the game room found it,
an old door somebody had painted
meticulously with an image
of David Bowie from the cover
of "Heroes." Bowie was half-bowing,
half saluting. Yes, the pounding slow depressing
beat of the title song set in Cold-War
Berlin, the melding of minds with Brian Eno
intensifying the insanity and burnout.
Who had painted it? Who had dared
in Tuscaloosa, Alabama,
in the late Seventies? Anywhere
but in that building, in its society
of zoological strangeness,
it would have been burned, beaten in,
not just deposed and embalmed.
Suddenly, the slogan promoting the album
Fires up my memory: *The Future belongs
to those who can hear it coming.*
I didn't hear it as the future, though;
"Heroes" seemed the last hurrah
of creation, vestige of a past
I'd been cheated of: I burned with cureless
envy of David's Golden Years.

Embraceable You (solo piano arrangement)

I recall the night
when I received the greatest
compliment of my performing life:
Sebastian, who'd foreseen disaster
and urged me not to perform,
saying, in his lightly Dutch English,
"Well, who would have thought
somebody could play
the piano so well
after so much *booze* and *pot*?"

Long Shadows at Noon

The sun has reached the inside end of the rug
near the sofa, the shadows have nothing
to do with the trees: they seem just to be there.
No longer refuges from the sun, I step in
and out dazzled, wishing the warmth would
linger past three p.m. Do animals
that hibernate have hangovers in the spring?

Ten Things Missing

I went back to the Heart of Dixie
and this time it wasn't funny
it overcame me I was damaged   sick
        the forests were gone to lumber
and the Christmas Tree Industry
the churches were warehouses or hangars

the kindest person in my family
        was dead   felled in his driveway
by the north wind   over-drawn by work
and fifty years with a wife
        who defied all good medicine

the snow danced around his body
but it would not stick by him

I was coughing, coughing to get it out
yes something was sticking in my lungs
        my throat   my ears maybe
it was the home cooking straight from the Piggly Wiggly

only the guava rum I found could burn
the taste away   so I kept filling the cup
and it never went empty

this is the Word of the Lord

Ode on a Line from Bryan Ferry

Every drop of blood is the same; you can never shed enough.
    —"The Name of the Game"

GIVE THE GIFT OF LIFE, say the bloodmobiles
all over town, but the Red Cross won't take my blood:
compromised by subtle extractions—
bleeding heart, anemia. ("Such a sensitive
child," my teachers clucked.)
                              "Must have
a tapeworm," my older brother blurted out
with all the sangfroid of a college boy
born in Nineteen Forty-Two, who still said
"Pardon my boardinghouse reach" at dinner—
a full-blooded man with golf clubs, baseball bats,
and wooden Don Budge tennis rackets,
none of which he taught me how to use.

I keep on bleeding, continue being pale
under a Florida August sun
with the blood collectors always
wanting more and rejecting it.

Florida

Elizabeth Bishop thought it was
the prettiest name for a state (What
would be the ugliest?) and here we are,
plenty of big trees almost choking
with locks of Spanish moss—no, they are
hair extensions—and sunshine on my whimsy.
(Oklahoma? Utah? Alabama? You
can tell by the way people say them
that a foul taste rises under the tongue.)
This corner is farthest from Key West,
where Bishop lived, just as small,
without the six-toed cats and giant spiders
that somehow make her town exotic
and half-habitable. Don't blame the state:
this dead flower comes straight from my heart.

June Afternoon, Florida

It's only after I hear the thunder from outdoors
that the computer spits out its noises,
a Premium Severe Weather Report.
I wait for the two o'clock storm,
a bracing, menacing early tea.
After a minute, the leaves, limbs,
and Spanish moss have grown
so waterlogged that they
seem ready to slide off the trees,
mint for a Gargantuan julep.

One Heart

It isn't hard to master the art of losing.
I Googled one thing but forgot another
While I was deep in the act of schmoozing.

I found a friend while schmoozing
but he found liquid pastures with another;
I can't even say what I was losing.

One year I found no solace e'en in boozing,
for Providence decided to take my mother.
I saw that nothing could be of my own choosing.

I found a needle; it took my blood and left me woozy,
yet still I worried most about my brothers
so deathly afraid was I of losing.

Still, it's evident that I have mastered losing,
though I'd stop now if I'd my druthers.
At least I've gotten back the joys of boozing,
for, at forty-eight, we'll go no more a'cruising.

Summer 1983

I am in Tuscaloosa, Alabama,
doing what? Sleeping in my old room,
now Grant's room, with its prospect
of the President's white-pillared mansion—
a morality tale of beauty and slavery,
the moral of which is never clear.
The sun exacts its stunning revenge
and the window units never rest;
the roar of frogs and locusts,
as if they've all rehearsed for years.
We wake at 2:00 p.m., drink amaretto;
Grant smokes his morning cigs.
(He'd ice a smoker now, you know.)
The Japanese are here to learn English;
we teach them to stretch "damn" and "shit"
into four syllables apiece.
After a night dancing with Masahiko,
I puke copiously in the driveway
of the University Club.
I buy a drawing of an attic
with this motto: "His former shelf...
shadow of his former shelf."
I am barely alive and loving it,
I am drunk with love of the South
and its merciless insanity....
But it is no longer mine.
(You don't believe me?)
My own cousins would kill me on a dare.

Locked Away

Early seventies: summer afternoons
at swimming pools and long rides home.
The music is very catchy, very bad—
Hamilton, Joe, Frank, and Reynolds'
"Don't Pull Your Love out on Me Baby,"
"Brandy," by Through the Looking Glass,
or "Family of Man," by Three Dog Night.
My brother-in-law is driving; sometimes
he lets us drive. He is morally
far too lax for my parents' tastes;
my first real drunk will be his doing.
At home, the air-conditioners
make a delicious aural womb; they mute
my father's carping, querulous voice.
I sleep and dream I'm in a cage,
lying next to a beautiful father.

The other night, in bed with Leonardo
I saw he was the man half...seen
and half-created in that puerile dream.
But when we had quelled our agitation
we began to talk, we dressed, we walked.
Heaven yawned as before.
Keith Richards sang "I Oughtta Be Locked Away."

I will never make a home
unless it be a palace and a prison,
a spare theme with serious variations.
Only good fathers may live in it
and they are each other's children.
Who are they? How many years away?

About the Poet

David Allen Case was born in Birmingham, Alabama, on July 15, 1961. He earned a Bachelor's degree from the University of Alabama and a Ph.D. in English from UCLA. From the mid-80's through 2011, he taught at several institutions of higher learning, including UCLA, Los Angeles City College, Pasadena City College, Glendale Community College, and Santa Fe College in Gainesville, Florida. He died unexpectedly at age 49 in Gainesville. Case's first book, *The Tarnation of Faust*, was published posthumously by Gunpowder Press in 2014. The publication of *Before Traveling to Alabama* further highlights Case's remarkable talent and marks the tenth anniversary of the Press, which, but for his poetry, would not exist.

ALSO FROM GUNPOWDER PRESS

Mother Lode, poems by Peg Quinn
Raft of Days, poems by Catherine Abbey Hodges
Unfinished City, poems by Nan Cohen
Original Face, poems by Jim Peterson
Shaping Water, poems by Barry Spacks
Mouth & Fruit, poems by Chryss Yost
The Tarnation of Faust, poems by David Allen Case

CALIFORNIA POETS SERIES
Downtime, poems by Gary Soto
Speech Crush, poems by Sandra McPherson
Our Music, poems by Dennis Schmitz
Gatherer's Alphabet, poems by Susan Kelly-DeWitt

ALTA CALIFORNIA CHAPBOOK SERIES
On Display, poems by Gabriel Ibarra
Sor Juana, poem by Florencia Milito
Levitations, poems by Nicholas Reiner
Grief Logic, poems by Crystal AC Salas

SHORELINE VOICES PROJECT
*Big Enough for Words: Poems and Vintage Photographs
from California's Central Coast*
David Starkey, George Yatchisin, and Chryss Yost editors

While You Wait: A Collection by Santa Barbara County Poets
Laure-Anne Bosselaar, editor

To Give Life a Shape: Poems Inspired by the Santa Barbara Museum of Art
David Starkey and Chryss Yost, editors

What Breathes Us: Santa Barbara Poets Laureate, 2005-2015
David Starkey, editor

Rare Feathers: Poems on Birds & Art
Nancy Gifford, Chryss Yost, and George Yatchisin, editors

Buzz: Poets Respond to SWARM
Nancy Gifford and Chryss Yost, editors

GUNPOWDER PRESS
BARRY SPACKS POETRY PRIZE

2015
Instead of Sadness, poems by Catherine Abbey Hodges
Selected by Dan Gerber

2016
Burning Down Disneyland, poems by Kurt Olsson
Selected by Thomas Lux

2017
Posthumous Noon, poems by Aaron Baker
Selected by Jane Hirshfield

2018
The Ghosts of Lost Animals, poems by Michelle Bonczek Evory
Selected by Lee Herrick

2019
Drinking with O'Hara, poems by Glenn Freeman
Selected by Stephen Dunn

2020
Curriculum, poems by Meghan Dunn
Selected by Jessica Jacobs

2021
Like All Light, poems by Todd Copeland
Selected by Lynne Thompson

2022
Accidental Garden, poems by Catherine Esposito Prescott
Selected by Danusha Laméris